Dinosaurs

Dougal Dixon

KINGFISHER

First published 2010 by Kingfisher
This edition printed 2013 by Kingfisher
an imprint of Macmillan Children's Books
a division of Macmillan Publishers Limited
20 New Wharf Road, London N1 9RR
Basingstoke and Oxford
Associated companies throughout the world
www.panmacmillan.com

Illustrations by: Peter Bull Art Studio
Additional illustrations by: Steve and Sam Weston;
Russell Gooday and Jon Hughes/Pixel Shack

ISBN 978-0-7534-3490-1

Copyright © Macmillan Children's Books 2010

3 5 7 9 8 6 4 2
2TR/1213/UTD/WKT/128MA

A CIP catalogue record for this book is available from
the British Library.

Printed in China

Picture credits

**The Publisher would like to thank the following
for permission to reproduce their material.
(t = top, b = bottom, c = centre, l = left, r = right):**

Psihoyos; 30cr Shutterstock/Jurjan Mosin; 30br
Shutterstock/Anton Foltin; 31 Shutterstock/slowfish

Contents

More to explore

On some of the pages in this book, you will find coloured buttons with symbols on them. There are four different colours, and each belongs to a different topic. Choose a topic, and follow its coloured buttons through the book, and you'll make some interesting discoveries of your own.

For example, on page 7 you'll find a red button, like this, next to a pack of hunting dinosaurs. The red buttons are about food and feeding.

Food and feeding

There is a page number in the button. Turn to that page (page 22) to find a red button next to another dinosaur eating something. Follow all the steps through the book, and at the end of your journey you'll find out how the steps are linked, and discover even more information about this topic.

Science

Dinosaur lives

Nature

The other topics in this book are science, dinosaur lives and nature. Follow the steps and see what you can discover!

What were dinosaurs?

The dinosaurs were a group of reptiles that lived between 230 and 65 million years ago. They were the most important land animals during the Triassic, Jurassic and Cretaceous periods of Earth's history.

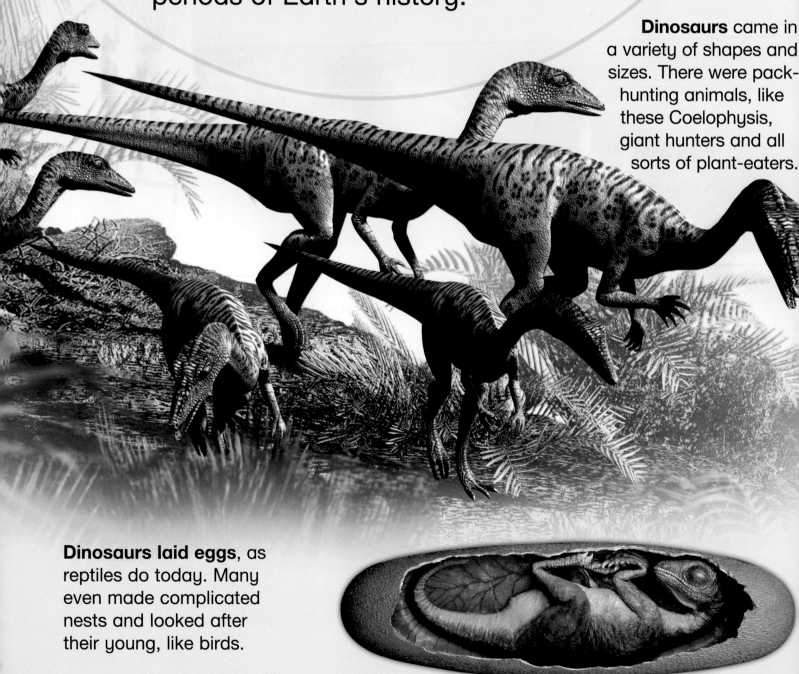

Dinosaurs came in a variety of shapes and sizes. There were pack-hunting animals, like these Coelophysis, giant hunters and all sorts of plant-eaters.

Dinosaurs laid eggs, as reptiles do today. Many even made complicated nests and looked after their young, like birds.

Triceratops lived at the end of the Cretaceous period.

The Cretaceous period (120 million years ago to 65 mya) saw the last of the dinosaurs. All kinds of armoured and horned dinosaurs appeared.

Jurassic times (180 mya to 120 mya) were the dinosaurs' heyday. Large meat-eaters evolved, and the long-necked plant-eaters became the biggest land animals ever.

Diplodocus was a Jurassic plant-eater.

Many dinosaurs had scaly skin.

These leathery, dinosaur-like scales belong to a modern crocodile.

By the end of the **Triassic period** (208 mya) there were all kinds of dinosaur groups, including the first big plant-eaters.

Plateosaurus was an early plant-eater.

Today's reptiles, like this gecko, have **legs** that stick out to the side. Dinosaurs held their legs beneath their heavy bodies.

The earliest dinosaurs appeared in the late Triassic period around 230 mya. They were swift two-footed hunters.

Eoraptor was one of the first dinosaurs.

What is this?

1 Diplodocus, a big plant-eater

2 Allosaurus uses its claws to kill and to tear meat.

3 Allosaurus, the bigges Jurassic meat-eater

Page 15

Meat-eaters

Today, meat-eating animals eat plant-eating animals. It was exactly the same in dinosaur times. In the Jurassic period, about 150 million years ago, fierce meat-eating dinosaurs were hunting all over the world.

A pack of hungry Ceratosaurus settles down to eat its kill – a baby Diplodocus. But then a giant Allosaurus leaps in to chase them away and steal the meal. While the fight rages, a swift little Ornitholestes nips in and snatches away a tasty piece of meat.

This is the big killing claw of an Allosaurus.

Fierce killers

If you look at a dinosaur skeleton, you can usually tell straight away if it was a meat-eater. Look for long jaws with sharp teeth, and clawed hands. You'll see strong back legs for running and a small body balanced by a heavy tail.

Back is held level, so that the teeth and claws are well forward.

Hands and claws are held inwards for seizing.

The teeth at the side of Albertosaurus jaws (above top) were flat blades, like steak knives, for cutting meat. Those at the front (above) were thicker, for holding on to struggling prey.

The meat-eating dinosaurs are called theropods.

Giganotosaurus was one of the largest of all meat-eaters. Over 12 metres long, it could attack and kill the biggest of the plant-eating dinosaurs in Late Cretaceous South America.

Allosaurus

stiff, heavy tail
for balance

Meat-eaters had three-clawed toes.

Allosaurus was
the biggest of the
Jurassic meat-eaters.
It stalked the plains
of North America,
attacking giant
plant-eaters,
or stealing
the prey killed by
smaller hunters.

Strong hind legs
carried the whole of
the dinosaur's weight.

Meat-eater skulls had flexible jaws
that could open wide and swallow huge
chunks of meat. Some were heavy and
worked like hammers, bringing the upper
teeth crashing down with killing force.

Ceratosaurus skull

Allosaurus used both its teeth and its claws for killing.

Jurassic giants

The heaviest, longest and tallest animals ever to have lived on land were the sauropods. These plant-eating giants spent most of their days eating, munching through enormous amounts of food. They had long necks and tiny heads.

Page 23

1 Diplodocus, a very long sauropod

2 Diplodocus eating leaves with its rake-like teeth

3 monkey-puzzle tree, a typical Jurassic tree

? This is a close-up of a young cycad leaf, a favourite food for sauropods.

The plains of Jurassic North America are dry places. Trees grow only along river banks and around lakes. The ground is covered by low-growing ferns and cycads. Big sauropods roam the landscape, eating this vegetation. Pairs of tall Brachiosaurus browse the high branches, like giraffes. Other sauropods feed on the middle branches or close to the ground.

Page 22

What is this?

3

4

5

6

4 Camarasaurus, the most common Jurassic sauropod

5 Brachiosaurus, one of the tallest sauropods

6 Brachiosaurus eating high branches

Plant-eating machines

The long-necked sauropods, the biggest land animals that ever lived, were all plant-eaters and ate huge amounts of food. We can tell a lot about these dinosaurs from fossils of their long necks, stomach insides and teeth.

Some sauropods had spines down their backs and clubs on their tails.•••

A scientist builds a model of a sauropod skeleton.

A Diplodocus skeleton shows its tail held off the ground and its neck held low. When it was alive, both were pulled up by strong tendons along the backbone.

Diplodocus was the longest-known sauropod.

A sauropod had an elephant-like body, four massive legs, a tiny head on the end of a long neck, and a long tail.

Shunosaurus

So much food passed through such a tiny mouth that the sauropod had no time to chew.

conifer needles

Huge amounts of **leaves and conifer needles** made up a sauropod's diet.

Sauropods swallowed **stomach stones**, which stayed in their stomachs and helped grind up tough plant food.

A sauropod's teeth were peg-like or spoon-shaped, good for raking leaves and twigs from branches, not for chewing.

Brachiosaurus had a tall neck, like a giraffe. Its long vertebrae (neck bones) lifted its tiny head to the highest trees, where its spoon-shaped teeth could scrape off leaves and twigs.

A group of Parasaurolophus look up suddenly. Their leader is making a loud trumpeting noise. It may mean danger, or he may be warning them away from other duckbills nearby.

Crested dinosaurs

In the late Cretaceous period, from about 100 million years ago to 65 million years ago, plant-eating dinosaurs called duckbills, or hadrosaurs, were a common sight. Many had strangely shaped crests on top of their heads.

4. Parasaurolophus baby with small crest

5. Parasaurolophus male bellowing

6. female with curled head crest

What is this?

3

6

5

Page 30

4

Page 23

Page 26

This is a jawful of new teeth ready to grow to replace those that get worn down.

Calls and colours

In today's world a lion roars, a cock crows and a peacock shakes its tail – all are ways that these animals use to communicate with one another. It was the same with dinosaurs. The duckbills could communicate both by sound and by visual signals.

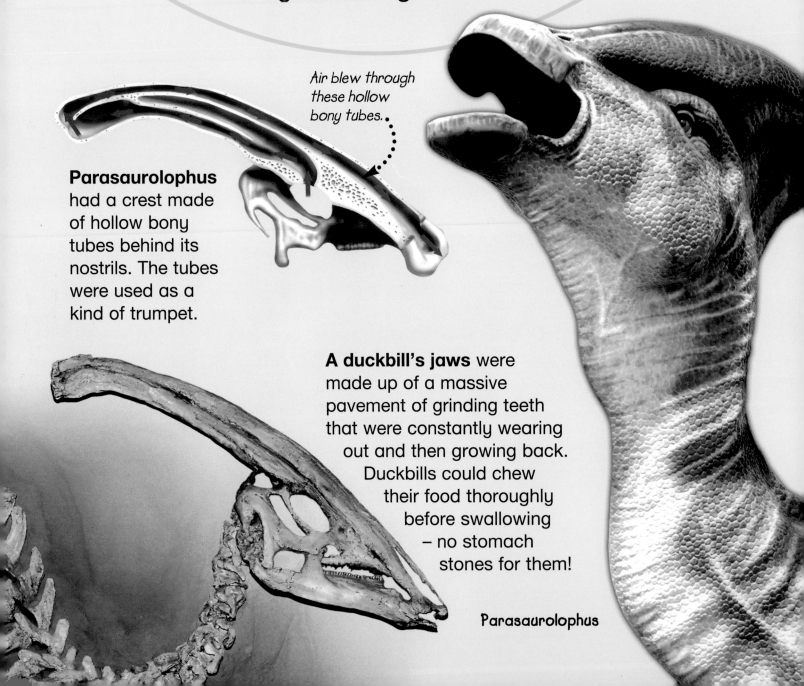

Air blew through these hollow bony tubes.

Parasaurolophus had a crest made of hollow bony tubes behind its nostrils. The tubes were used as a kind of trumpet.

A duckbill's jaws were made up of a massive pavement of grinding teeth that were constantly wearing out and then growing back. Duckbills could chew their food thoroughly before swallowing – no stomach stones for them!

Parasaurolophus

Dinosaur colours were probably quite bright, but we don't really know. Duckbills may have had striking patterns so that they could identify one another, or they may have been camouflaged.

Anatotitan could have been this colour...

...or this colour.

The sound made by a Parasaurolophus was probably like a trumpet or trombone.

Sometimes we find fossilized duckbill skin.

Although we know the skin texture, we can only guess the colour.

Tsintaosaurus had a crest that stuck straight up like a unicorn horn.

Olorotitan had a hatchet-shaped crest.

Different duckbills had different crests. Like the horns of antelopes today, the crests helped duckbills to identify the animals that were like them and belonged to their own herds. As well as the different shapes, the crests would have had a range of colours, making each species really distinctive.

Corythosaurus had a semi-circular crest like an ancient Greek helmet.

Dinosaurs with armour

With so many big, fierce meat-eating dinosaurs around, it is no wonder that some of the plant-eaters evolved armour to defend themselves. Horns, plates, neck shields and spikes all appeared on different dinosaurs.

1 Albertosaurus, a fierce predator

2 Edmontonia, protected by back armour

3 tail weapon of blade-like spikes

? This is part of a Styracosaurus skull. The gaps in the neck shield stop it being too heavy.

4

5

Page 15

An Albertosaurus is hunting. It ignores the herds of horned dinosaurs – there are too many of them. Instead it attacks a lone Edmontonia, and is not put off by its armour and spikes.

6

What is this?

4 Einiosaurus (left) and Triceratops in the distance

5 Styracosaurus facing danger as a group

6 Styracosaurus with neck shield and horn

Stegosaurus had a double row of plates sticking up along its back. These might have been brightly coloured and used for showing off, but it also had two pairs of spikes at the end of its tail – a serious weapon.

Stegosaurus's plates were probably covered in skin.

Stegosaurus had armour studs in its neck to protect its throat.

heavy tail club made of lumps of bone

Under attack!

Dinosaur life was an arms race! As meat-eaters became bigger and fiercer, the plant-eaters needed more and more elaborate armour in order to defend themselves. Plant-eating dinosaurs had heavy armour made up of different combinations of plates, shields, studs, clubs and vicious horns.

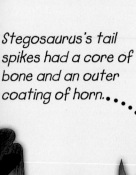

Stegosaurus's tail spikes had a core of bone and an outer coating of horn.

Pachycephalosaurus had a bony dome on its head. This was used not just for fighting enemies. Big males would have fought each other to be leader of the herd.

bony head dome used as a battering ram

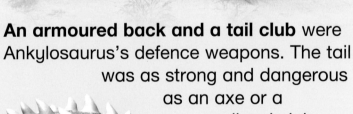

An armoured back and a tail club were Ankylosaurus's defence weapons. The tail was as strong and dangerous as an axe or a medieval club.

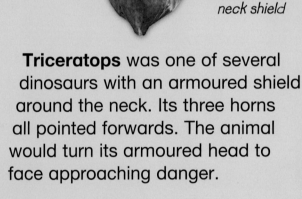

thick, bony neck shield

Triceratops was one of several dinosaurs with an armoured shield around the neck. Its three horns all pointed forwards. The animal would turn its armoured head to face approaching danger.

Triceratops herds may have formed a circle to protect their young.

1 herd of Maiasaura

2 Troodon parent defending its nest

3 Chirostenotes stealing an egg

Page 15

Page 10

Dinosaur nests

Like their descendants, the birds, dinosaurs laid their eggs in nests. They had to defend their eggs and young from all kinds of attack. Many dinosaurs nested in large groups, and, when the young grew big enough, moved around in herds for protection.

What is this?

Page 27

4

5

Page 19

6

Troodon, a small meat-eater, sits on its nest. It is part of a large group, or colony, all nesting together beside a lake during the Cretaceous period. Bigger dinosaurs, like the duckbill Maiasaura, nest in a colony nearby. All the time the dinosaur parents have to guard against egg-stealers such as Chirostenotes.

Troodon had feathers very much like these, which belong to a modern eagle.

Growing up

We know quite a lot about dinosaur life. Some lived alone, while others lived in family groups and herds. Fossil eggs and nests tell us about their early lives, and footprints show where they travelled. Sometimes fossils of whole herds are found.

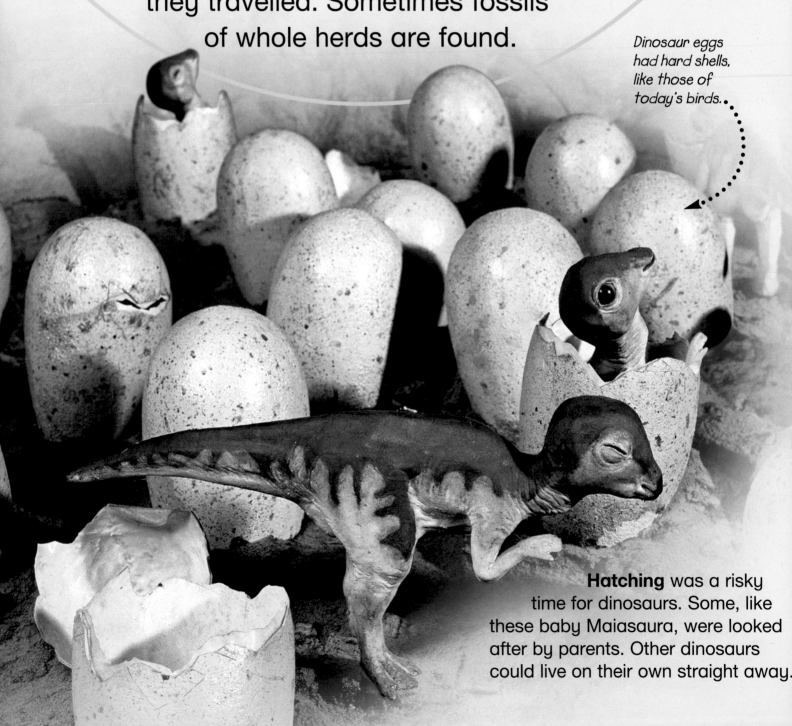

Dinosaur eggs had hard shells, like those of today's birds.

Hatching was a risky time for dinosaurs. Some, like these baby Maiasaura, were looked after by parents. Other dinosaurs could live on their own straight away.

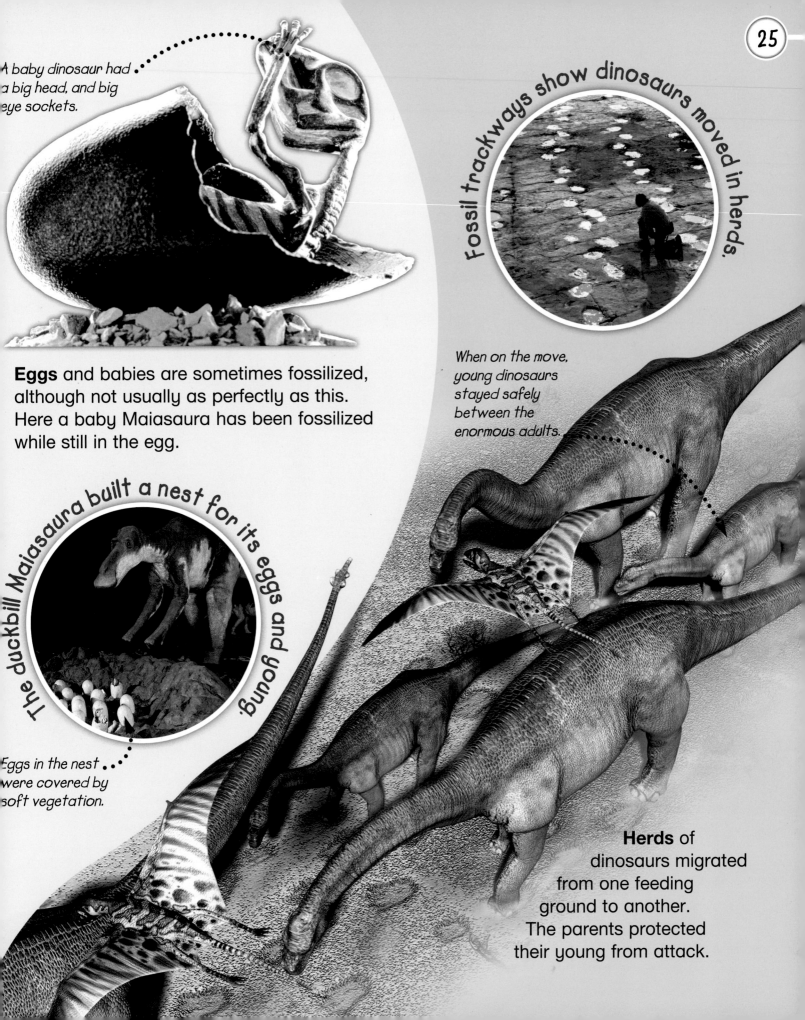

A baby dinosaur had a big head, and big eye sockets.

Eggs and babies are sometimes fossilized, although not usually as perfectly as this. Here a baby Maiasaura has been fossilized while still in the egg.

The duckbill Maiasaura built a nest for its eggs and young.

Eggs in the nest were covered by soft vegetation.

Fossil trackways show dinosaurs moved in herds.

When on the move, young dinosaurs stayed safely between the enormous adults.

Herds of dinosaurs migrated from one feeding ground to another. The parents protected their young from attack.

Page 30

What is this?

1 Volcanic gases add to the damage.

2 Triceratops, a plant-eater, faces starvation.

3 Quetzalcoatlus, a flying reptile, will die out.

What happened?

Suddenly, 65 million years ago, all the dinosaurs vanished. We think that a giant meteorite struck the Earth and caused so much damage that the dinosaurs could not survive. Around 50 to 80 per cent of all animal and plant life died out too.

Page 30

3

4

5

Page 30

A meteorite hurtles through the atmosphere. A few seconds later it will hit the Earth and explode, killing everything nearby. Dust and steam thrown up will change the climate for many years. This will kill the plants and cause the death of plant-eating animals and then of meat-eaters.

6

❓ This is a duckbill's beak. It is made of horn with a sharp edge, used for scraping twigs and leaves.

The story so far

Sometimes a dead dinosaur would fall into a river and be buried by sand. Over time the sand would turn to rock and the bones to mineral. Millions of years later, that rock might be worn away by the weather, revealing the fossil. Only then can we find it.

Some flowering plants survived when dinosaurs died out.

Around 65 million years ago, the dinosaurs became extinct (died out), along with three-quarters of all other animal species. Afterwards a new set of animals evolved and repopulated the Earth.

the meteorite impact

Palaeontologists are scientists who study the ancient life of the Earth. Through their work we can find out about the animals and plants of long ago – including dinosaurs.

palaeontologists uncovering a sauropod skeleton

Finding a whole dinosaur skeleton is rare. More often the remains are incomplete, and some dinosaurs are known from only a single bone.

Discovering dinosaurs in a museum is great fun. But a mounted skeleton is the result of years of careful excavation and study.

A dinosaur in a museum is usually made from the parts of different skeletons.

Dinosaur fossils are not made of the original bone – that has been replaced by mineral.

These boxes contain fossilized dinosaur dung.

Dinosaur remains are taken to a laboratory to be studied. Different palaeontologists are experts in different types of fossils. Some study bones, while some study footprints or even dung.

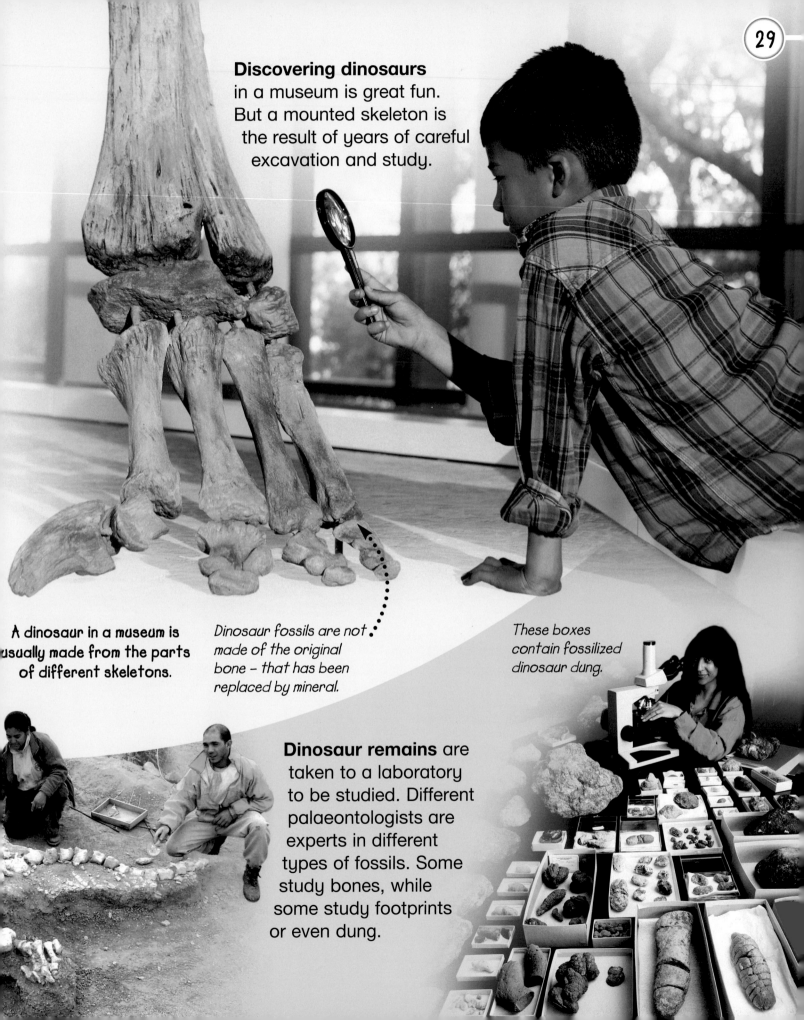

Ceratosaurus on the attack

Some **meat-eaters** hunted alone. Others hunted in packs. Small and medium-sized hunters, such as Ceratosaurus, would have found it easier to hunt big prey in groups.

Eggs are a very nutritious (energy-rich) food. Some meat-eating dinosaurs, such as Chirostenotes, probably robbed other dinosaur nests.

Chirostenotes

Food and feeding

At the start of the age of dinosaurs, Earth's **plants** were mostly ferns and conifers. There was no grass. By the end of the dinosaur age, broadleaved trees had evolved.

Dragonfly

Insects were some of the first land creatures. They evolved 200 million years before the dinosaurs appeared. Today there are several million species of insects.

Nature

Many dinosaurs **lived in herds** for protection against meat-eaters. They migrated from one feeding ground to another as the seasons changed.

We know that at least some dinosaurs built **nests**, laid eggs and looked after the youngsters when they hatched – just like birds do today.

a duckbill's nest

Dinosaur lives

long-necked Brachiosaurus

If scientists find a complete dinosaur **skeleton**, they can see straight away what the animal looked like. More often they find just part of a skeleton, or bones scattered about.

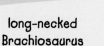

Fossilized footprints give us clues about dinosaur life – whether they ran or walked, and how many of them moved about together. It is impossible to tell what dinosaur made what footprint, though.

Science

More to explore

Diplodocus, a sauropod

Sauropods ate plants. They were a bit like vacuum cleaners, standing in one place while their long necks hosed around for food.

Tyrannosaurus, one of the biggest and the last of the meat-eaters, had jaw muscles that were powerful enough to crush all your bones, and a mouth big enough to swallow you whole.

There were many other types of **reptiles** living in the age of dinosaurs. Crocodiles, turtles and the ancestors of all modern lizards, like this one, scuttled around the dinosaurs' feet.

Mammals appeared when the dinosaurs did. Throughout dinosaur times they were small and insignificant. Only when the dinosaurs died out did they become the most important animals on Earth.

Cimolestes

Some dinosaurs had clever ways of **defending** themselves from predators. Styracosaurus probably crowded together so that their horns and shields could protect the whole herd.

Styracosaurus

Dinosaurs could hear well and they could also see well. Some, like the duckbills, could **communicate** to one another using visual displays and loud noises.

Sometimes we find fossils of **dinosaur skin**. Then we can see if the animal's surface was scaly or leathery, or even feathered.

meteorite

Scientists study the **extinction** of the dinosaurs by looking at the rocks of the time – rocks full of meteorite dust, damage from tsunamis and layers of charcoal from forest fires.

Index

In this index, each dinosaur name has a pronunciation guide in brackets.